DATE DUE		
NOV 9 1992		
SEP 2 8 1993		
NOV 8 1993		
NOV 5 1994		

Billings County Public School
Dist. No. 1
Medora, North Dakota 58645

DEMCO

THE EXXON-VALDEZ OIL SPILL

by
Tom Schouweiler

LUCENT
B·O·O·K·S

WORLD DISASTERS

These and other titles are available in the Lucent World Disasters Series:

Library of Congress Cataloging-in-Publication Data

Schouweiler, Tom, 1965-
  The Exxon-Valdez oil spill / by Tom Schouweiler
  p.   cm. — (World disasters)
  Includes bibliographical references and index.
  Summary: Examines the impact of the 1989 Exxon-Valdez oil spill on the environment and people of Prince William Sound and describes the steps taken to minimize the damage and prevent a recurrence.
  ISBN 1-56006-016-6
  1. Oil spills—Environmental aspects—Alaska—Prince William Sound Region—Juvenile literature. 2. Tankers—Accidents—Environmental aspects—Alaska—Prince William Sound Region—Juvenile literature. 3. Exxon Valdez (Ship)—Juvenile literature. [1. Oil spills— Alaska—Prince William Sound Region. 2. Tankers—Accidents. 3. Exxon Valdez (Ship)] I. Title. II. Series.
  TD427.P4S36 1991
  363.73'82'097983—dc20   91-29499
                                                                CIP
                                                                 AC

10222

© Copyright 1991 by Lucent Books, Inc.
Lucent Books, Inc., P.O. Box 289011, San Diego, California, 92198-0011

Table of Contents

Preface
The World Disasters Series

World disasters have always aroused human curiosity. Whenever news of tragedy spreads, we want to learn more about it. We wonder how and why the disaster happened, how people reacted, and whether we might have acted differently. To be sure, disaster evokes a wide range of responses—fear, sorrow, despair, generosity, even hope. Yet from every great disaster, one remarkable truth always seems to emerge: in spite of death, pain, and destruction, the human spirit triumphs.

History is full of disasters, arising from a variety of causes. Earthquakes, floods, volcanic eruptions, and other natural events often produce widespread destruction. Just as often, however, people accidentally bring suffering and distress on themselves and other human beings. And many disasters have sinister causes, like human greed, envy, or prejudice.

The disasters included in this series have been chosen not only for their dramatic qualities, but also for their educational value. The reader will learn about the causes and effects of the greatest disasters in history. Technical concepts and interesting anecdotes are explained and illustrated in inset boxes.

But disasters should not be viewed in isolation. To enrich the reader's understanding, these books present historical information about the time period, and interesting facts about the culture in which each disaster occurred. Finally, they teach valuable lessons about human nature. More acts of bravery, cowardice, intelligence, and foolishness are compressed into the few days of a disaster than most people experience in a lifetime.

Dramatic illustrations and evocative narrative lure the reader to distant cities and times gone by. Readers witness the awesome power of an exploding volcano, the magnitude of a violent earthquake, and the hopelessness of passengers on a mighty ship passing to its watery grave. By reliving the events, the reader will see how disaster affects the lives of real people and will gain a deeper understanding of their sorrow, their pain, their courage, and their hope.

Introduction

Untold Environmental Destruction

Shortly past midnight on March 24, 1989, the fully loaded *Exxon Valdez* oil tanker slowly moved away from the Alaskan port of Valdez and headed into Prince William Sound. The tanker was so heavy that it hung five stories beneath the surface of the water. On the bridge, Capt. Joseph Hazelwood radioed the Coast Guard and requested permission to leave the outgoing sea-lane to avoid ice. The Coast Guard gave Hazelwood permission, knowing the expert seaman could easily complete the maneuver.

To avoid the ice, Hazelwood pointed the *Valdez* toward the dangerous rocks of Bligh Reef. He then told Third Mate Gregory Cousins to turn the ship back into the outgoing sea-lane and away from the reef at a certain point in the channel. After he gave the order, Hazelwood left the bridge.

If Cousins had started to turn when Hazelwood ordered, the *Valdez* would have successfully maneuvered out of the channel. But, for reasons unknown, Cousins did not start the crucial turn until seven minutes after he had been ordered to. Since it takes nearly two miles of open water for a tanker the size of the *Valdez* to complete any maneuver, the ship would be unable to turn in time. To their horror, crew members realized that the tanker was less than one mile away from Bligh Reef and moving directly toward it. There was no time to turn away. Powerless to stop

The Exxon-Valdez Oil Spill in U. S. History

1542
Spanish sailor Juan Rodriguez discovers oil near Santa Barbara, California

1741
Danish explorer Vitus Bering, sailing east from Siberia, lands in Alaska

1776
United States declares independence from Britain; British seafarer Capt. James Cook names Prince William Sound in Alaska

1854
First American oil company, Pennsylvania Rock Oil, formed

in New Haven, Connecticut

1859
First commercially productive oil well drilled near Titusville, Pennsylvania by Edwin L. Drake

1861-1865
American Civil War

1867
The United States purchases Alaska from Russia for $7,200,000

1914-1918
World War I

1939-1945
World War II

1959
Alaska becomes the forty-ninth state of the union on January 3

1967
U.S. tanker *Torrey Canyon* runs aground off Land's End, England, spilling nearly 35 million gallons of oil

1969
U.S. Congress passes National Environmental Policy Act requiring environmental impact studies before oil drilling or other projects that may damage the environment are begun

1970
U.S. government establishes

6

the impending disaster, the crew and Cousins watched the reef loom up out of the darkness.

There was a loud, scraping noise as the rocks of Bligh Reef sliced through the tanker's hull. Hazelwood, in his cabin, heard it at the same time that Cousins radioed for him to come back to the bridge. As Hazelwood stood aghast at the huge hole in the hull and the oil seeping out, he gave the order to stop the engines. He then radioed for help. Everyone on board watched helplessly as thousands of tons of oil—enough to fill a football stadium—oozed out of the damaged tanker.

Thousands of animals died on the first day. One local resident counted 650 dead birds on one beach alone. And many more did not even make it to the beach. Thousands of birds sank to the bottom of the sound. Otters tried in vain to rub the toxic oil out of their eyes and ears, swallowing the oil and freezing to death when their oil-soaked fur could no longer insulate them from the cold. The disaster also threatened the important Alaskan fishing industry. Those who fished for a living worked frantically to protect millions of recently hatched salmon from the deadly spill.

In the first crucial days following the disaster, chaos reigned. By the time everyone agreed on who should clean up the spill and how it should be done, a storm blew in, causing huge swells that churned the oil into a thick soup called mousse. In this form, the oil is impossible to collect with the cleanup methods available. Thousands of gallons of oily water slammed into the beaches surrounding the sound and the Valdez area.

It seems incredible that such a huge disaster began with a simple human error. What is even more incredible is that almost no one in Alaska, including the oil companies, the citizens, and the government, believed such a spill was likely.

Environmental Protection Agency
1973
Arab oil embargo drives up the price of oil in the West
1974
Construction begins on the eight-hundred-mile-long Alaskan oil pipeline from Prudhoe Bay to Valdez
1976
Spanish tanker *Urquiola* runs aground off the coast of Spain, spilling nearly 30 million gallons of oil
1977
U.S. tanker *Hawaiian Patriot* catches fire in the northern Pacific Ocean, spilling more than 29 million gallons of oil; Alaskan pipeline finished
1978
U.S. tanker *Amoco Cadiz* runs aground off the coast of France, spilling 65 million gallons of oil
1979
Ixtoc I oil well in southern Gulf of Mexico blows out, spilling more than 176 million gallons of oil; Burmese tanker *Burmah Agate* collides with another vessel in Galveston Bay, Texas, spilling more than 10 million gallons of oil
1989
Exxon Valdez runs aground and spills 11 million gallons of oil into Prince William Sound in Alaska, eventually contaminating more than one thousand miles of coastline
1990
Exxon Valdez captain Joseph Hazelwood found guilty of negligence, but acquitted of criminal mischief. Sentenced to 1000 hours of public service and a $50,000 fine
1991
United States leads United Nations forces against Iraq in the Persian Gulf War

One

Valdez and Prince William Sound

Valdez is a small coastal town located in the area of Prince William Sound, an isolated inlet on the southern coast of Alaska. Although Valdez is situated in an arctic region, a warm-water current from the Pacific Ocean called *Kuroshio* brings relatively warm weather during the frigid winter months. This unusually warm weather in an otherwise freezing climate attracts all kinds of wildlife and plants to Valdez and Prince William Sound.

Impenetrable forests of hemlock, spruce, and cedar cover the Chugach and Kenai mountains that ring the sound. Along the shoreline, narrow bands of alder, willow, and cottonwood trees stand. In the spring, flowers—including blue storksbill, pink columbine, and yellow snapdragons—appear near the water's edge.

The sound is home to many types of water mammals as well. Because its waters never freeze, the sound is a year-round home to sea lions, porpoises, seals, and over ten thousand sea otters. Humpback and killer whales also visit the sound in the course of their annual migrations. Numerous fish, including halibut, dogfish, and many kinds of salmon, also live in the sound.

Lastly, several rare and unusual types of birds nest and live in the deep forests near the sound's clear waters. The sound's abundant food and water make it an ideal place for swans, ducks, geese, loons, cormorants, puffins, murres, and bald eagles.

Although Northern Europeans did not settle in Alaska until the early nineteenth century, Prince William Sound and the town of Valdez have been populated by the Chugach-Aleut people for at least four thousand years. These early tribal people lived in small villages and hunted and fished for survival. Today, the ancestors of these original inhabitants still live in the Valdez area. Many are employed by the thriving fishing industry that began in the early nineteenth century.

Last Untamed Frontier

More than a hundred years ago, white settlers were attracted to Alaska because it was one of the last untamed frontiers. They quickly took advantage of Alaska's abundant fishing and started one of the first fish canneries in the Valdez

The port town of Valdez nestles between the Chugach Mountains and Prince William Sound on Alaska's southern coast.

A short-lived Alaskan gold rush swelled the population in the Valdez
area in the 1880s.

area. Fishing and fish canneries still play an important part in the Alaskan economy.

Gold Rush

In addition to the fishing industry, a minor gold rush attracted many settlers in 1880. Gold was discovered in the Gastineau Channel southeast of Prince William Sound, near the present site of the Alaskan capital, Juneau. Gold continued to be discovered in much of southeastern Alaska, and it was mined in a large area to the north of Valdez. For a time, the gold rush caused a large population increase in this area. As the gold supply dwindled, the population gradually tapered off in the 1920s. Eventually, white settlers returned to fishing as the chief source of income.

However, another of Alaska's natural resources eventually led to a booming new industry. After World War II, the U.S. Navy spent $60 million searching for new petroleum and natural gas fields on the North Slope of Alaska. The North Slope is the oil-rich land north of the Brooks mountain range, east from Icy Cape to the border of Canada. Geologists soon learned that 9.6 billion barrels of crude oil lay below the perpetually frozen ground of the North Slope, north of the Arctic Circle.

Less than Tempting

In the 1950s, no one was interested in drilling and pumping these oil reserves. Federal laws prohibited drilling for oil in Alaska's fragile wilderness. In addition, drilling in Alaska, where temperatures reached fifty degrees below zero Fahrenheit during the winter, would have been difficult and unpleasant. These difficulties, coupled with the fact that the United States could meet its petroleum needs without Alaska's oil and without importing oil from other countries, made Alaska's oil reserves less than tempting. So, although a few companies and individuals leased the land in hopes that it would someday be valuable, no drilling was attempted.

By 1970, however, these circumstances changed. The United States could no longer fill all its energy needs. It began to import oil from Saudi Arabia, Iraq, Iran, and Kuwait because their oil was less expensive and more readily available than oil from U.S. sources. Encouraged by the ease of buying oil from the Middle East, the United States allowed its dependence on foreign oil to grow. As U.S. industry and population increased, cheap foreign oil supported the country's growth.

Then in 1973, events changed U.S. attitudes toward foreign oil. The Middle Eastern countries that sold oil to the United States temporarily cut off supplies. The result was a shortage that led to gasoline

Motorists wait to get a share of the limited gasoline supply. The 1973 Arab oil embargo against the United States caused long lines at filling stations.

THE ENERGY CRISIS OF 1973

In 1970, the United States reached the peak of its oil production. Petroleum was being pumped from all known oil fields, except those of Alaska's North Slope. At the same time, demand for oil increased, and it became necessary to import oil to meet the demand. It was cheaper to import oil than to extract it from the cold and inhospitable North Slope.

Saudi Arabia, Kuwait, Iran, and Iraq exported inexpensive oil to the U.S. They, along with other Middle Eastern countries such as Syria, Egypt, and Libya, formed a coalition called the Organization of Petroleum Exporting Countries, or OPEC. OPEC still exists today. Its purpose is to allow the oil-producing countries of the Middle East to set standards for how much oil will be produced, how much that oil will cost, and to whom the oil will be sold.

OPEC was willing to meet U.S. oil demands until war broke out between Egypt and Israel on October 7, 1973. The countries of OPEC were enemies of Israel, and all were angered by the fact that the United States was supplying the Israeli army with arms and money.

As a result, OPEC immediately cut its production by 5 percent, and threatened to continue cutting production by 5 percent each month until the United States withdrew its support from Israel and used its influence to return Egyptian territory occupied by Israel. OPEC also cut exports of oil to most countries in Europe.

It was during this cutoff, or embargo, that gas became scarce. Long lines waited outside gasoline stations. Gas was rationed. Prices soared as the supply dwindled.

In November and December of 1973 the U.S. secretary of state, Henry Kissinger, successfully negotiated the end of the conflict between Egypt and Israel. After the conflict was resolved, many of the OPEC countries were anxious to reestablish production at full capacity. These countries lost money when they were not able to sell oil. On the other hand, they wanted to protest the United States' continued support for Israel.

On December 23, 1973, OPEC met and raised the price of oil from its October 1, 1973, level of $2.59 per barrel to $11.65 per barrel. The people of the United States were shocked and dismayed by this huge increase in price and the realization of how dependent they were on other countries. The government responded by increasing efforts to find a supply of petroleum within the United States. It was then that the frozen North Slope of Alaska became important and the Trans-Alaska Pipeline was proposed.

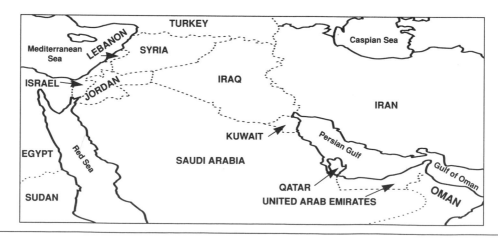

rationing and long lines at gas stations. During the winter, some schools in the midwestern United States had to close on cold days because of a lack of heating oil. This was the first time many Americans realized how dependent on Middle Eastern oil the United States had become.

Alyeska

In response to this crisis, the U.S. and European oil companies who had leased land on Alaska's North Slope formed a group, or consortium, called Alyeska. Alyeska consisted of large corporations such as ARCO, British Petroleum, and Exxon, together with several smaller companies. They wanted to drill for oil in Alaska. Alyeska hoped that it could persuade the government to revoke the laws protecting Alaska's environment and help the United States reduce its dependence on Mideast oil. Together these companies began to explore the possibility of drilling and transporting Alaskan crude oil to the lower United States for refining.

Environmentalists protested drilling for oil in such a fragile place. They argued that the ecosystem in a cold environment is more delicate and harder to repair than an ecosystem in a warmer area. Although these arguments were compelling, U.S. energy needs took precedence over Alaska's environment.

On July 17, 1973, the U.S. Congress voted to allow drilling on Alaska's North Slope. Congress also authorized the construction of a

The eight-hundred-mile-long Alaskan oil pipeline carries almost two million gallons of oil a day from Prudhoe Bay in the north to Valdez in the south.

pipeline to run south from drilling sites to the city of Valdez. Building on the pipeline began in spring 1974 and was completed in 1977. The first oil through the pipeline reached Valdez on July 28, 1977. The port of Valdez was expanded to accommodate the huge ships that came to collect the oil.

Millions of Gallons a Day

Since the pipeline opened, almost two million gallons of oil have moved through it each day to storage tanks atop the hills near the port of Valdez. To ship the oil to the United States, large hoses from the storage tanks are connected to oil tankers, and gravity then sends the oil into the ships. The ships that

HISTORY OF ALASKA AND PRINCE WILLIAM SOUND SINCE 1741

In 1741, the Danish explorer Vitus Bering was the first European to sail near the waters of Prince William Sound. In the service of the Russian czar Peter the Great, Bering sailed eastward from Siberia. His ships landed on Kayak Island, slightly more than a hundred miles from the present site of Valdez.

Prince William Sound was not discovered by Europeans, however, until 1778. On May 12 of that year, English navigator James Cook sailed into the bay and named it Prince William Sound after the son of King George. While in the sound, he and some of his crew went ashore and met some of the natives.

Around this same time, explorers from France, Spain, and Russia explored the area, hoping to take advantage of the wealth of sea otter skins. These skins were highly valued for use in clothing in the late eighteenth century.

Because its territory of Siberia was so nearby, Russia successfully established settlements in the area. In 1792, Russian traders and soldiers seeking to establish a settlement in the sound, fought with the natives on Hinchinbrook Island.

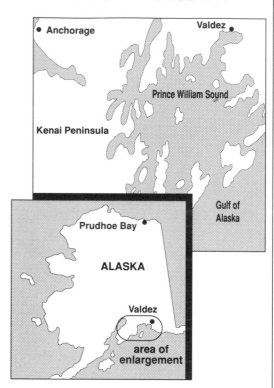

English explorer Capt. James Cook found Prince William Sound in May 1778 and named it after the son of the king of England.

One year later, after defeating the natives, the Russians established a settlement called Port Etches. Trade in seal and sea otter pelts was conducted from there and throughout Alaska by a Russian organization known as the Russian-American Company.

The Russian-American Company hunted seals and otters until the 1860s, when catches fell off and the company began to lose money. Russia agreed to sell Alaska to the government of the United States. On March 30, 1867, for the sum of $7,200,000 (less than twelve cents an acre), the United States bought Alaska from Russia.

With the discovery of gold in the Klondike of nearby Canada, the city of Valdez was established and grew rapidly. It served as a way station for those who rushed to the region in the late nineteenth century.

carry the oil are called supertankers. Supertankers are the largest moving vessels ever created. Some can hold up to three hundred thousand tons, or over two million barrels, of crude oil.

The pipeline and the oil industry quickly gained importance for the people of Valdez and for all Alaskans. In order to quiet fears that the oil companies would harm Valdez and the neighboring sound, Alyeska agreed to return a share of all profits made from Alaskan oil to the state of Alaska. This money amounts to a lot for the people of Alaska. From 1978 to 1980, the money was used to build new hospitals, schools, roads, and community buildings. In 1980, oil companies supplied enough money to the state government that the state income tax was eliminated. Additional money was refunded to Alaskans. In 1988, this refund amounted to $826.93 for each adult and child in the state. The oil companies also provide many jobs along the pipeline and especially in the port of Valdez.

At first, the fishers who docked in Valdez were concerned that the huge oil tankers would reduce their catch by polluting the water and killing the fish. This threat never materialized, and the fish were unaffected by the presence of the tankers. In fact, fishers were expecting the best salmon catch ever in 1989. For twelve years, small fishing boats and massive oil tankers coexisted peacefully, in the sea and in the port of Valdez. Soon, however, the harmony between the oil and fishing industries would change.

Two

Recipe for an Oil Spill

After the completion of the Alaskan oil pipeline, the oil industry in the Valdez area grew enormously. Huge oil tankers regularly crowded the waters of Prince William Sound. The presence of these oil tankers worried local fishers and citizens. What would happen if there were a large oil spill? How would it be cleaned up? In response to these concerns, three groups—the oil industry, the Coast Guard, and Alyeska—agreed to take measures to increase tanker safety and to prepare for oil spills.

Members of the oil industry, who own and operate the oil tankers, promised to decrease the possibility of a spill by building double-hulled ships. In a single-hulled tanker, one layer of steel separates the oil inside the ship from the water outside it.

In a double-hulled tanker, two layers of steel and a strong metal framework are used. It's as if a smaller ship were placed inside a larger one. A double-hulled tanker is much more likely to survive a collision without a spill. This is because an object can penetrate the first hull, but still leave the second hull intact.

Coast Guard Takes Precautions

The U.S. Coast Guard also took steps to ease worries about an oil spill. The Coast Guard agreed to help prevent and to help clean up oil spills in the sound. To make it safer for ships to negotiate the narrow sea-lanes of the sound, the Coast Guard set up a radar tracking station in Valdez. Ships moving through the sound were tracked on radar to ensure that they remained clear of other ships and hazards in the water, such as ice. The Coast Guard trackers also made sure the tankers remained in waters deep enough to keep them from running aground.

In addition, the Coast Guard was responsible for inspecting Alyeska's operations at the Valdez oil-loading terminal. The Coast Guard made sure that oil was being loaded onto the ships safely. Before sailing, ships were checked to make sure all their navigational, steering, and emergency equipment was in working order. If the Coast Guard found a ship that was unsafe, it was not allowed to sail.

The Coast Guard also maintained two fully equipped "strike teams" to

The Bottom Line — Single or Double Hulls?

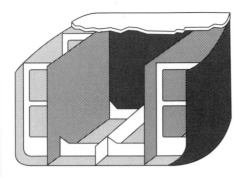

Single Bottom

A sheet of metal about one-inch thick separates the oil from the ocean.

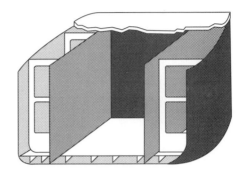

Double Bottom

Two metal sheets are separated by an empty compartment about ten-feet high. In the case of grounding, only the bottom sheet would rupture.

Double Hull

Double bottoms and double sides provide the maximum protection against groundings and collisions.

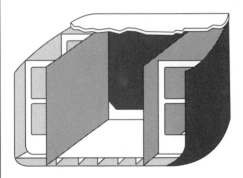

Partial Double

Only part of the tanker has a double bottom. This design enables the tanker to carry a load of oil along with other materials that do not require a double bottom.

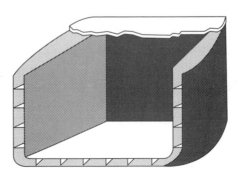

Source: The Tanker Register, U.S. Coast Guard and the Tanker Advisory Center.

react to oil spills. These teams were trained to assess oil spills, coordinate the gathering of cleaning equipment, and supervise the cleanup if necessary. One team, stationed in the Atlantic, was located in New York City. The other team operated in the Pacific and was located in San Francisco. Each was responsible for patrolling its entire coastline.

Alyeska's Safeguards

Even though the tanker owners and the Coast Guard were prepared to prevent or assess oil spills, Alyeska was responsible for responding to and organizing cleanup efforts after a spill. Though the company that owned the oil would ultimately be held responsible for the expense and the cleanup efforts, members of Alyeska agreed to have a team that could take charge immediately after a spill.

To ensure a quick response, Alyeska maintained a spill-readiness team. Alyeska's team was prepared twenty-four hours a day, and could be at the site of a spill within five hours. They had a ship full of oil-cleaning equipment, including boom lines, mechanical skimmers, and chemical dispersants.

Alyeska claimed that the spill-readiness team could handle a spill of up to two hundred thousand barrels. An average-sized oil tanker carries around a million barrels. But in most oil spills, only a fraction of the oil on the ship leaks into the water, so Alyeska believed its team could handle any spill likely to occur.

As time passed without a major oil spill, the high standards of safety established when the pipeline was new were not maintained. All three groups—the oil companies, the Coast Guard, and Alyeska—became less and less equipped to deal with a spill as time went on.

The oil industry, which had promised to begin building double-hulled tankers, experienced economic hardships in the early 1980s. As a result, double-hulled tankers were not built. Oil companies argued that the tankers were too expensive. If the companies were forced to build them, they would have to raise prices. In this highly competitive field, raising prices would mean that American oil companies could not compete with foreign oil. So oil companies used their existing tankers longer. Rather than replacing a tanker after ten years, they used it for fifteen and twenty years. And when new ones were built, they had only one hull. Since the oil companies were not required by law to build double-hulled tankers, no federal agency was able to force them to fulfill their promise.

Reduced Crew Size

The same economic difficulties that prevented oil companies from building safer tankers also led them to cut the size of the ships' crews. Crew members were replaced by computers. Ships' officers were assigned additional clerical duties and paperwork. In 1977, when the pipeline was completed, average tanker

A ship's navigator uses radar, a computer, and telecommunications to safely maneuver his vessel into port. Computerized ships have enabled oil companies to reduce the size of their crews.

crews numbered around forty sailors. In 1989, the same size tankers had crews of twenty or less. Because of these small crews, twelve- to fourteen-hour workdays were normal for tanker crew members. Because of the long hours, many sailors left the oil-transport industry altogether.

The Coast Guard was also affected by a lack of money. Its oper-

ating budget, supplied by the federal government, was cut back in the early 1980s. This meant that equipment deteriorated, and fewer people were assigned to the Valdez Coast Guard station.

Budget cutbacks reduced the effectiveness of the radar station in Valdez as well. The radar that had been installed in the early days of the pipeline was replaced by a unit ards such as ice and submerged rocks. In addition, crews monitoring the radar were reduced, and the radar was sometimes unattended during shift changes.

More important, Coast Guard personnel cutbacks reduced the number of people available to inspect operations at the Valdez oil terminal. With staff greatly reduced, ships were no longer inspected every time they left the port. Instead, they were checked only occasionally. As a result, owners of the tankers let safety standards decline as the risk of an inspection also declined.

Alyeska gradually cut back the measures it had taken to ensure fast response to an oil spill as well. In 1982, Alyeska assigned the members of the spill-readiness team to other duties within the oil-loading terminal. The team was no longer standing by twenty-four hours every day. Instead, members would respond to a call and assemble on board the spill-cleaning ship. This increased the time it took the team to respond to a call.

Taxed to Limit by Small Spill

The team's equipment grew old and was not replaced. The equipment had run down so much that the team was no longer prepared to clean a large spill. In January 1989, the tanker *Thompson Pass* leaked 1,670 barrels of crude oil into Prince William Sound through a gash in its hull. The team, which was supposed to be able to handle a spill up to 200,000 barrels, was

that was not as strong. Ships were often lost for short periods of time on the new radar. The downgrading of the radar system made it more possible for ships to stray from the established shipping lanes near haz-

Two months before the *Exxon Valdez* spill, the tanker *Thompson Pass* leaked nearly seventeen hundred barrels of oil into Prince William Sound. Even this relatively small spill severely taxed the poorly prepared cleanup team.

taxed to its limit by the small spill. Cleaning even this small spill was such a strain on the equipment that afterwards the equipment was unloaded from the ship and the ship was brought up on land for repairs. While the boat sat waiting for repairs, the equipment was left on land. The spill-readiness team was clearly no longer prepared to take on a major oil spill.

Many people believe that the oil companies, the Coast Guard, the Alaskan government, and the citizens of Alaska became complacent about safety precautions. After all, in 1989, it had been twelve years since the pipeline was built, and no major spill had occurred. Even environmentalists began to relax, be-

cause the oil industry had not caused any environmental damage.

All of these problems would combine toward catastrophe the night the supertanker *Exxon Valdez* prepared to begin its final journey. On March 23, 1989, Capt. Joseph Hazelwood boarded the *Exxon Valdez* after a day of shore leave in the city of Valdez. Scheduled to leave for California at 9:00 P.M., the ship was loaded with forty-five million gallons of North Slope crude oil. This oil was to be refined into gasoline, jet and diesel fuel, fuel oils, and other petroleum products at refineries on the west coast of the United States. But it would never arrive at its destination.

Three

Collision with a Reef

At 9:00 P.M. on March 23, 1989, the *Exxon Valdez* started out from the port of Valdez, steered by a local harbor pilot, a sailor employed by Exxon who is especially familiar with the port and whose job it is to take ships safely out of it. A light rain fell in the darkness of night.

On the bridge with the harbor pilot were Capt. Joseph Hazelwood and Third Mate Gregory Cousins. Hazelwood waited to take the wheel from the harbor pilot. He had spent at least part of the day ashore drinking at a Valdez tavern called the Pipeline Club. This was against Exxon policy. But Hazelwood did not appear to be drunk.

Two shipping lanes exist in Prince William Sound. One is for ships coming into Valdez and the other is for ships leaving the port.

At 11:15 P.M., the harbor pilot boarded a small boat and left the *Exxon Valdez*. Shortly afterward, Hazelwood radioed the Coast Guard that he was turning the ship into the incoming lane in order to avoid floating ice in the outbound lane. The Coast Guard okayed the move, which pointed the ship at the dangerous rocks of Bligh Reef. Soon afterward, unknown to the crew of the *Exxon Valdez*, the Coast Guard lost the ship on radar. Knowing that Hazelwood was an excellent sailor and familiar with the waters of the sound, they were confident that he would straighten the ship's course before hitting the reef.

Hazelwood planned to keep the ship turned until it reached the incoming lane and then to straighten its course. That way, he could avoid the ice and maintain his speed of ten knots. It was the last maneuver of Hazelwood's career.

With paperwork to do, Hazelwood turned the wheel over to Gregory Cousins and left the bridge at approximately 11:50 P.M. He went to his quarters nearby after telling Cousins to begin to turn the ship slightly to the right at a hazard light near Busby Island to bring it back into the shipping lane.

Delay Put Ship Off Course

The ship reached the light near Busby Island at 11:50 P.M., but Cousins did not begin to turn the ship until seven minutes later. This delay put the ship off course, out of the shipping lane and heading toward Bligh Reef, whose jagged

An oil tanker cautiously threads its way along one of two shipping lanes in Prince William Sound as it heads out to the Gulf of Alaska.

rocks lay just below the water's surface. The mistake was discovered by the watchman up on deck, who ran down from his post to the bridge to report that the ship was off course. He had spotted the light to alert ships of the presence of Bligh Reef. Cousins realized that the ship was not doing what Captain Hazelwood intended it to do and that it was outside the safe shipping lane.

He responded by ordering a "counter rudder maneuver." The counter rudder movement was intended to turn the ship sharply, in this case to bring it back into the shipping lane and away from the rocks of Bligh Reef. This is done by turning the rudders sharply, causing the ship's stern to swing and turn the ship in the desired direction.

The counter rudder movement was initiated by the rudder helmsman, Robert Kagan, and the huge ship began to turn. A few minutes later Hazelwood, in his quarters, felt the ship jolt. Cousins had been too late. The ship could not change course quickly enough. "I think we're in serious trouble," Cousins told Hazelwood over the phone. Hazelwood ran to the bridge.

Collision

At 12:04 A.M. on March 24, the *Exxon Valdez* collided with Bligh Reef. The ship's massive steel structure creaked and groaned as the sharp rocks of the reef tore it open. In minutes the ship slowed, then stopped. Oil began to pour out of the ship so fast it made six-foot oil swells. Oil gushed out of the tanker at a rate of 233 gallons per second and spread rapidly. Frantically, Hazelwood slowed the engines to steady the ship on the reef. Reversing the engines and pulling the ship off the reef would have ripped the gash in the ship's hull even larger and caused the ship to sink or capsize. Hazelwood kept the engines running in order to keep the ship pushed up against the reef.

"Fetched Up Hard"

After securing the ship as well as he could, Hazelwood radioed the Coast Guard. His distraction showed in the 12:27 A.M. radio broadcast, "We've . . . it should be on your radar there . . . we've fetched up hard aground north of Goose Island off Bligh Reef. And, uh . . . evidently . . . leaking some oil, and we're going to be here for a while."

The Coast Guard notified Alyeska of the spill, and the fifty workers that made up the spill-readiness team were called into action. With their ship on land for repairs, some of the team searched frantically for another. Others dug through the snow to reach the cleaning equipment that had been unloaded and stored near where their ship lay in dry dock.

Another ship was quickly located, and the team spent the rest of the night and the whole morning moving the equipment onto it. Fourteen precious hours passed as the team slowly loaded each piece of equipment onto the new ship.

By 2:30 on Friday afternoon,

when the team arrived at the spill, a tremendous amount of oil had spilled and spread from the crippled tanker. The small ship deployed boom line in an attempt to stop the spreading oil.

The oil hemorrhaging from the tanker was too much for the little ship to handle. There was not enough boom line to contain the spill, and wherever the line was laid down, oil washed over or under it. The Coast Guard commander from Valdez, Steven McCall, flew over the oil spill in a helicopter that afternoon. Viewing the spreading oil slick and the boom line in the water, he remarked:

> [The boom line] looked like small yellow worms in a big pool of oil. When I realized the boom was actually a mile long, the immensity of the problem struck home. We were in trouble as far as the eye could see.

After unsuccessfully trying to contain the oil on the first day of the spill, Alyeska turned responsibility over to Exxon. Exxon spent the second day of the spill surveying the damage and assembling cleanup crews, ships, airplanes, and helicopters. Exxon began hiring hundreds of Alaskans to help with the cleanup. Most of these people were owners and crews of fishing boats, who knew the waters of the sound.

Fortunately, the winds blew calm, and oil spread slowly from the ship. A slight breeze from the northeast moved the oil away from the mainland near Bligh Reef. Cleanup coordinators frantically tried to get cleanup teams onto the sound while the good weather lasted. Exxon wanted to take advantage of the calm seas to apply the new chemical dispersants.

Coast Guard as Watchdog

As Exxon readied its equipment, however, the Alaskan state government and the federal Environmental Protection Agency protested. They did not trust Exxon to have a free hand at cleaning up the spill, possibly causing more damage.

Oil flows out past containment booms designed to prevent its spread.

10222

They asked Coast Guard commander Steven McCall to evaluate the risk of the chemical dispersants. McCall allowed Exxon to spray on a small experimental area. Using the dispersants on the larger spill, McCall argued, was too risky. The damage to the environment, especially to salmon and other fish that swim where the oil would collect, was potentially too great. As a result, chemical dispersants were not used during the first two crucial days after the spill.

The oil slick grew each day. Two days after the spill, oil engulfed Naked Island, leaving miles of its beaches covered with black oil. Some cleanup crews and equipment were on the waters, working around the clock to contain the oil and skim it off the surface. But the oil spread too quickly.

McCall realized that the spill was becoming uncontrollable. So, on the third day, Sunday, McCall reversed his decision and authorized spraying over the entire spill. Unfortunately, as the planes were being loaded with chemical dispersants, a spring storm blew up. Its high winds kept the airplanes grounded. The stormy winds also changed the nature of the spilled oil. The large and violent waves whipped the oil into a foamy substance called mousse. When oil is in mousse form, it does not mix with chemical dispersants. So the opportunity to use chemical dispersants had been lost. It would also be extremely difficult to pick up the mousse with the mechanical skimmers because oil in that form does not stick to the absorbent belt.

The high winds produced another dangerous side effect. The oil slick began to spread more quickly, traveling toward the Kenai Peninsula, the mainland to the southwest

---

THE SPILL AND THE SPREAD OF OIL

Bligh Reef is twenty miles away from the port of Valdez, at the end of the narrowest part of the channel that leads out of Prince William Sound.

During the oil spill, winds carried the oil southwest toward the Kenai Peninsula. Naked and Smith islands were the first to be hit and received the greatest amount of oil on their beaches. But even these two islands were not completely saturated by oil. Where it washed ashore, oil collected in areas ranging in size from less than a mile to up to ten miles. The southeast sides of the islands, out of the path of the spilled oil, stayed clean.

Unfortunately, the spill occurred just before the herring and salmon seasons would have begun. As the oil covered more and more of Prince William Sound, Alaskan state officials feared that fish would be killed in great numbers and that any living fish caught would be contaminated by the oil. They closed the herring season and reduced the salmon take. Nonetheless, the salmon harvest was better than the year before, and few contaminated fish were found.

The oil continued to spread and collect along the Kenai and Alaskan peninsulas. The last of it washed ashore 550 miles from Bligh Reef, almost two months after the *Exxon Valdez* ran aground.

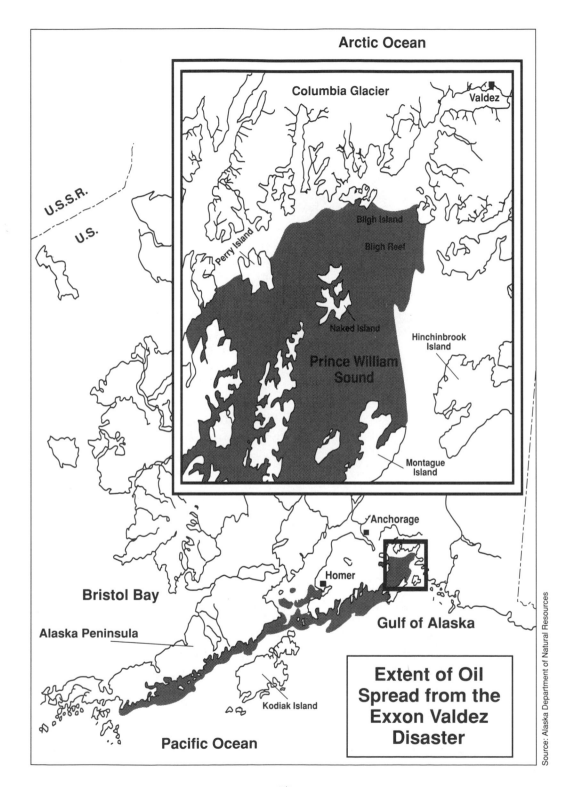

Arctic Ocean

Columbia Glacier

Valdez

U.S.S.R.

U.S.

Bligh Island

Bligh Reef

Perry Island

Naked Island

Hinchinbrook Island

Prince William Sound

Montague Island

Anchorage

Homer

Bristol Bay

Gulf of Alaska

Alaska Peninsula

Kodiak Island

Extent of Oil Spread from the Exxon Valdez Disaster

Pacific Ocean

Source: Alaska Department of Natural Resources

of Bligh Reef. The oil could then cover hundreds of miles of shoreline. By Sunday night, the oil slick had spread over a thirty-mile area.

On the fifth day of the spill, Tuesday, oil had surrounded and soiled much of the shorelines of Green, Knight, and Montague islands, and began to wash ashore on the Kenai Peninsula, fifty miles away from Bligh Reef. The oil began to thicken into a gummy tar. It coated shorelines, seabirds, and otters. Oil also washed ashore at Herring Bay on Knight Island, where pregnant seals go to molt and bear their young. As their oil-covered mothers died, orphaned seals uttered humanlike cries on the blackened shores.

Thousands of birds died as well. Some suffocated as they were engulfed by oil six inches thick. Some were so coated with oil that they sank into the water and drowned.

(above) Thick globs of heavy, black oil wash ashore along Prince William Sound and kill thousands of seals, otters, and seabirds. (below) A local fisherman inspects the oil-fouled beach where the carcass of a gray whale has washed up.

OIL SPILLS AND AQUATIC LIFE

Oil spills have a disastrous effect on plant and animal life. Especially vulnerable are benthic organisms—plants and animals that live on or near the sea bottom. According to an organization called the National Research Council (NRC) the greatest harm in an oil spill occurs to life on the seafloor, like seaweeds or clams.

One example of this effect is the spill from the barge *Florida*. It ran aground in Buzzards Bay, Massachusetts, on September 16, 1989, and spilled 630 tons of refined oil. Researchers documented that small fish and benthic animals were killed immediately. In lightly oiled sites, these animals recovered in one year. In heavily oiled sites, the animals had still not completely recovered ten years after the spill.

In a marshy area called Wild Harbor, where the *Florida* spill migrated, even greater damage was done. After the spill, 77 bushels (over 2,400 quarts) of dead soft-shell clams, and 11,200 bushels (almost 360,000 quarts) of hard-shell clams were collected. Twelve years after the spill, when the study ended, recovery in this area was not yet complete.

On March 16, 1978, the *Amoco Cadiz* spilled 223,000 tons of light crude oil when it ran aground in the English Channel near Portsall, France. Crabs, barnacles, and sea urchins perished immediately. Beaches were "littered with dead animals," according to the report. The results were so disastrous in some areas that, according to the NRC, "several decades plus active conservation measures may be required for return to prespill conditions."

The tanker *Arrow* ran aground in Chedabucto Bay in Nova Scotia, Canada, on February 4, 1970. Much of the oil passed through animals that live near the surface of the water to the sea bottom in the form of fecal pellets. As a result, some plants were killed off completely and had not reappeared six years later. Benthic animals such as clams were killed in large numbers, and did not grow as quickly after the spill as before. Ten years after the spill, oil was still visible in seafloor sediments.

Studies made of these and other oil spills revealed that oil is most dangerous in shallow water, where organisms live in high concentration. Especially vulnerable are marshy areas, where the abundance of plant life makes cleanup impossible. Plant and animal life almost always recover from the effects of the spilled oil, although this process takes longer in cold climates.

A fisherman unloads the day's catch of bushels of clams. Clams live on the seafloor and are especially vulnerable to spilled oil that sinks to the sea bottom.

Still others died from exhaustion and starvation, unable to fly or feed themselves in the middle of the huge oil slick. On Green Island alone, a thousand dead and dying birds were counted. Roy Corral, a freelance photographer on board one of the cleanup vessels around the islands, witnessed the spill:

> It's incredible. The oil is in every nook and cranny of those islands. It has splashed ten feet up on the rocks. The seabirds are covered with oil and they're about ready to die. I saw dozens and dozens of dead seabirds—murrelets, ducks, cormorants, loons—and . . . seals, all covered in oil.

Sea otters suffered similarly. Normally, an otter is kept warm by its fur, which it grooms constantly. The grooming stimulates glands that secrete an oil, called sebum, that insulates the otter from the harsh cold. But, when the otters were covered with oil, their fur lost its insulating quality, and they quickly froze to death in the frigid spring waters of Prince William Sound. Otter biologist Lisa Rotterman watched from a helicopter as oil washed over a group of sea otters sleeping in the water: "A blob of oil hit them, and we saw them struggle and become totally immersed. There was that terrible feeling of helplessness." An accurate count of the dead animals was never made, since otters, unlike birds, sink when they die in the water. Many animals died in the early days of the spill because there were

Members of the cleanup crew on Prince William Sound inspect the frozen, oil-soaked body of a sea otter drowned by the Exxon oil spill.

not enough rescue workers.

While Exxon was mobilizing cleanup and animal rescue crews at a frantic rate, the oil spread just as quickly. It was impossible to clean or even contain it. Too much oil streamed into the water too quickly, and the winds moved the slick at a rate of ten miles a day. Exxon was not prepared for a spill this large. Many residents of Prince William Sound were outraged with the time it took Exxon to clean the oil and save birds, seals, and otters. Riki Ott, a fisher and biologist, visited the site of the spill. She was struck by two things:

> One was the smell. It just about knocked you out. And the other thing was, where was everybody? I mean, this was a big spill, and *where was everybody?* I couldn't believe it.

Fishers like Ott were upset about the apparent lack of activity, because fish hatcheries were threat-

(above) The natural beauty of the Alaskan forest stands in stark contrast to the poisoned, black shores of Prince William Sound, awash in oil from the *Exxon Valdez* spill. (below) A wildlife rescue worker examines a dead, oil-covered bald eagle to determine if oil caused its death.

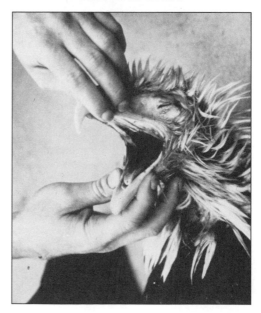

ened by the spreading oil. A hatchery is a place in the sea where the eggs of fish are hatched and where the fish are protected until they are old enough to seek food for themselves. Because fishing is so important in Alaska, there are many herring and salmon hatcheries located around Prince William Sound.

The oil spill occurred at a bad time for these fish. The young, called fry, were about to be released into the waters of the sound to feed on microscopic animals called plankton. Plankton is most numerous in late April or early May. Salmon fishers were worried that the oil might kill both the plankton and the salmon fry. Fearing that Exxon crews might arrive too late, fishers organized to protect the hatcheries themselves. With money supplied by Exxon, they obtained boom line and skimmers to keep

SALMON AND THE FOOD CHAIN

When oil spilled into Prince William Sound, fishers' immediate concern was how the spill would affect the salmon. Their concern was magnified by the fact that the spill happened in the early spring, when the phytoplankton begin to grow.

Phytoplankton are minute plants that multiply at an astronomical rate in the early spring as the water warms. The phytoplankton are then fed upon by the zooplankton—microscopic animals that multiply rapidly as their food source expands. The zooplankton are in turn eaten by the pink salmon fry. The young salmon and other small fish become food for larger organisms such as larger fish, seabirds, otters, bears, eagles, sea lions, and people.

Because the phytoplankton are at the base of an important food chain, scientists such as ornithologist Pete Mickelson were concerned about how the spill would affect their growth in the early weeks of the spill. Mickelson was concerned that the oil might kill the phytoplankton, causing a ripple effect all the way up the food chain—contaminating "phytoplankton at the base of the food chain [and building] up in high organisms that ingest it."

Although many members of this food chain were killed by spilled oil, scientists have found that too few were killed to permanently impair it. Some speculate that the food chain could be back to prespill conditions as early as 1994.

An Alaskan fisherman displays his catch. Salmon, an important part of the ecology and economy of Alaska, were threatened by the *Exxon Valdez* oil spill.

A worker at the San Juan salmon hatchery near Prince William Sound reports to a government monitor on the status of the hatchlings. Fishing crews worked feverishly to protect the salmon fry at the hatchery from falling prey to the Exxon oil spill.

the oil from reaching the young fish.

One hatchery, the San Juan salmon hatchery in Sawmill Bay, was threatened by oil on the fifth day of the spill. Fishing boats and their crews used booms to form a series of barriers around the hatchery. Between the booms they ran skimmers to pick up oil that leaked through. Though the conditions were not ideal for the use of skimmers, the operation was successful. Most of the 117 million pink salmon fry were saved from the oil.

While the young salmon were being protected, the Alaskan government cancelled the opening of the herring season and restricted the adult salmon take for fear that the fish populations, already damaged by the spill, might be further damaged by overfishing. Exxon promised to make up the difference in cash to any fisher who did not catch as much as in previous years.

The oil continued to spread. There was simply not enough boom line or skimmers, which were only partially effective on the thick brown mousse, to halt the spread of oil. One witness, commenting on the ineffectiveness of the boom line, said that the *Exxon Valdez* "needed to have a dam built around it." Only one week after the spill, the oil slick extended ninety miles from Bligh Reef and coated miles of shoreline along the Kenai Peninsula. It could not be stopped.

Four

Aftermath

Except at the San Juan and a few other fish hatcheries, where fishers made valiant efforts, the oil that leaked out of the *Exxon Valdez* was not collected. Instead it washed up along hundreds of miles of shoreline. Exxon, under criticism for its inability to remove the oil from the water, began the largest ever oil cleanup effort on the beaches of the sound. Don Corbett, Exxon's Alaska public affairs manager, promised that Exxon would "pick up, one way or another, all the oil that's out there. . . . We hope to leave Prince William Sound the way we found it."

Exxon initiated a massive beach-cleaning effort. Out-of-work fishers, housewives, and fortune seekers from Anchorage and Juneau, and later from the lower forty-eight states, streamed into Valdez for cleanup jobs. The positions paid up to $16.69 per hour, and included lodging and food. Most of these people washed oil off the rocks along soiled beaches.

Fishing boats, not in use because of the spill, were chartered to bring workers to and from the beaches, to transport food, and to collect dead and dying animals. Hundreds of people worked on the beaches in protective suits and gloves.

Some workers sprayed the rocks with hot, pressurized water. The hot water washed the oil off the rocks and into the sea. Although this procedure made the beaches appear cleaner, most of the time the hot water just forced the oil into the gravel and under the surface, where it formed a thick tar. Also, the high temperature of the water killed tiny organisms that help degrade the oil. The result was that beaches appeared to be clean, but concealed large amounts of oil just below the surface.

A far more common way of cleaning the beaches was simply to wipe individual rocks with absorbent towels. Considering the more than one thousand miles of rocks that had to be cleaned, it seems incredible that this was the most used method.

Bioremediation

Another process that was tried very successfully on seventy miles of heavily oiled beaches was bioremediation. A fertilizer was sprayed on the beaches to stimulate the growth of naturally occurring bacteria. These bacteria degrade the oil and

Oil cleanup crews use pressurized hot water to wash oil off the rocks of the Prince William Sound shoreline. The method effectively cleaned the rocks but trapped the oil deep into the underlying gravel.

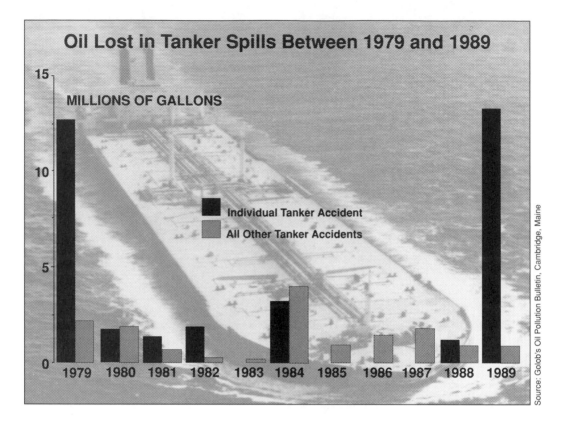

Source: Golob's Oil Pollution Bulletin, Cambridge, Maine

change it to a harmless substance.

When the bacteria are sprayed onto the oily rocks, they go deeper and deeper looking for oil to consume. The end result of the process is a dark substance that is not harmful to plants or wildlife. Chuck Costa, one of the site managers for the experiment, explained how the process worked: "We are still learning how deep the bacterial [cleaning] activity may go. We believe it may extend as deep as twelve inches in some areas. What the bacteria leave behind are asphalt hydrocarbons. They are unsightly, but they aren't toxic."

The bacteria, called Inipol E.A.P. 22, cleaned one beach in three weeks. Rocks were clean on top and bottom. Only a trace of the oil that coated the beach could be found five inches below the surface. Though the experiment was successful, it was not used more widely because it is not known what effect the bacteria in the fertilizer has on other life forms.

Cleaning the beaches was not the only concern for the thousands of people at work in Prince William Sound that summer. People worked feverishly to save wildlife as well. Thousands of otters and seabirds were covered with oil. Most of the animals affected died. Workers picked up oiled birds and otters and put them in plastic garbage

A BEACH-CLEANING PROCESS

All around Prince William Sound, crews worked with hoses, skimmers, and a variety of equipment to remove oil from the rocks of the shoreline. Although the equipment looked sophisticated, the tactics for oil pickup had not changed since the 1950s.

First, workers blasted oil off of the rocks. This was done with water heated on barges to a temperature of 140 degrees Fahrenheit. Workers on shore, wearing suits to protect them from both the heat of the water and from the oil, shot the hot water through high-pressure hoses.

Next, workers pumped seawater to the high ground above the oiled area. There it was run through perforated hoses so that it percolated down and carried the oil blasted off the rocks to the water's edge.

At the water's edge, more workers with hoses used cold seawater to flush the mix out to sea. In the water around the cleanup site, mechanical skimmers with oil-absorbing belts picked up the oil. Once the oil was aboard a ship, it was squeezed out of the belt and collected. That oil was later either recycled, burned, or sent to toxic waste dumps. Boom line surrounded the whole project, to prevent oil from escaping back out into the sound.

Other cleanup crew members transported equipment, workers, and supplies. Boom tenders, people whose job it was to keep the boom line intact, checked for breaks and oil seepage. And it was one person's job to stand on shore to keep a lookout for bears that normally come down to the shoreline to fish for food.

Though teams worked for six months, it is estimated that only 20 percent of the oil that washed up on the beaches was removed in this way.

A cleanup crew works on a piece of shoreline after the Exxon spill. The crew uses a combination of methods to wash off, sop up, and carry away the gooey gunk that surrounds them.

bags, fearful that other animals would scavenge the dead and ingest the lethal oil. Many bald eagles died this way. Kelsey Crago was hired by Exxon to locate dead birds:

> We've picked up about three thousand birds in the last five days. Most of them were murres, killed around the Barren Islands. . . . They keep drifting in with the tide. We're collecting the bodies to keep the bears and eagles from eating them.

Many times, birds were so completely immersed in oil that their identity was a mystery. However, some birds and otters, though cov-

ered with oil, were not dead. These were the focus of a huge rehabilitation effort.

Bathing Clinics

Both Exxon and volunteer organizations set up bathing and medical clinics in an attempt to save some of the animals devastated by the spill. Saving an animal—a bird or an otter—is a multistep process that takes weeks to accomplish.

Rescue workers went out on the sound in hundreds of small boats, called skiffs, to pull the injured animals from the water. Some were

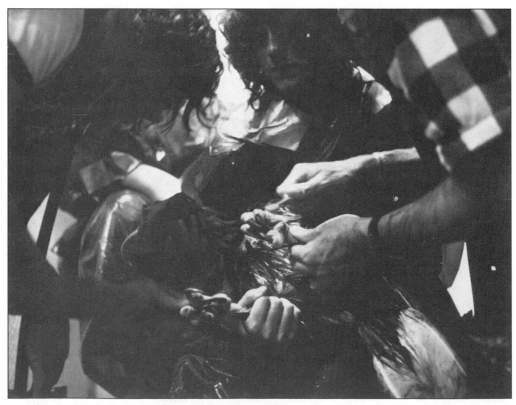

A volunteer uses a toothbrush to remove oil from a bald eagle's plumage. The eagle nearly drowned when it became soaked with oil while fishing above the oily waters of Prince William Sound.

HOW PETROLEUM AFFECTED WILDLIFE

Many animals, especially otters and seabirds, quickly drowned in the oil released by the *Exxon Valdez*. Others died from the side effects of the oil. The most common of these secondary effects was hypothermia. Hypothermia occurred when the oil destroyed the insulating qualities of fur or feathers, and animals froze to death.

Sea otters were especially vulnerable to the oil's effects. After ingesting oil while attempting to remove it from their fur, otters developed internal injuries including respiratory ailments and liver and kidney damage. These two organs—the liver and the kidney—are both used in processing what is taken into the body. The livers of the oiled otters became diseased from their bodies' efforts to remove the oil. The otters' livers were "almost crumbly," according to a veterinarian at one rehabilitation clinic.

Bald eagles, the national bird of the United States, were also hurt by the oil. As they fed on the carcasses of oiled animals, they also ate oil. In April, after learning of the huge potential damage to the eagle, Exxon added two trained capture teams and an eagle rehabilitation center in Anchorage.

Nonetheless, by mid-July of 1989, 109 dead eagles had been found. They died from ingesting the oil and from having oil soak their feathers and restrict flight. Worse, eagle reproduction was severely affected by the oil. Besides making eagles weak and unable to care for their young, crude oil also kills embryos or prevents them from maturing fully.

A sea otter froze to death in icy waters when oil saturated its protective fur.

healthy enough to evade capture, so rescue workers sometimes spent three hours in pursuit of just one bird. Many others, especially otters, were so near death that they could be picked up by hand.

After capture, animals were brought to a larger boat, usually an out-of-work fishing vessel, where they were placed in a box to be brought to one of the clinics. It took about twenty-four hours to fill a vessel with injured and dying animals. Many died before they even reached the clinics.

At the clinics, the incoming animals were assessed as to their chances for survival. Hopeless cases were injected with T-61, a pet euthanasia drug. Those judged capable of surviving were placed in boxes or cages covered with blankets to begin the arduous treatment process. Jessica Porter was the chief veterinarian at a bird-rehabilitation center located in the Prince William Sound Community College in Valdez. She explained the complexity of the process: "A lot of people seem to think they can bring an oiled bird into their house and put it in the sink, suds it up, and then

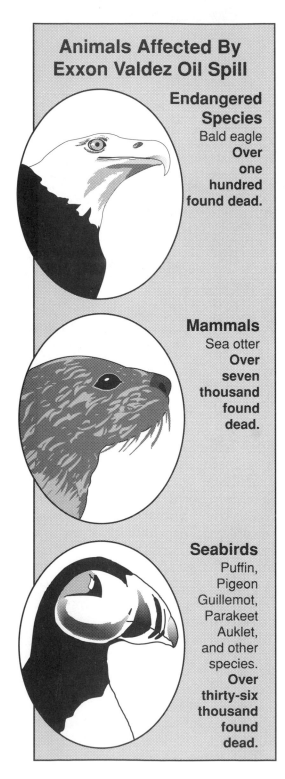

Animals Affected By Exxon Valdez Oil Spill

Endangered Species
Bald eagle
Over one hundred found dead.

Mammals
Sea otter
Over seven thousand found dead.

Seabirds
Puffin, Pigeon Guillemot, Parakeet Auklet, and other species.
Over thirty-six thousand found dead.

release it." The process, instead, is "a combination of bird husbandry, ornithology, veterinary medicine, and . . . chemistry."

Wildlife not only had to be cleaned. Many had swallowed toxic amounts of oil as they tried to clean themselves. Animals often suffered from internal injuries caused by oil. For this reason, oil was not removed from fur or feathers until an animal was stabilized. Tubes were put down the animal's throat, and a thin, watery mixture of food and chemicals meant to counteract the toxicity of the oil was forced into the stomach. The oily animals were left in boxes covered with cloth, and fed through tubes until they were strong enough to undergo the washing process.

Hypothermia and Death

Animals that survived the feedings were washed with great care, usually by people who did not normally work with wildlife. Bruce Adkins, a massage therapist, and Christy Huvinsky, a wood carver, even left their regular jobs to help rehabilitate birds. Adkins and Huvinsky worked as a team. They would first take a bird and submerge it in a tub full of soapy water. While Huvinsky held the bird, Adkins gently moved the water around the bird's body. He would gently rub the feathers for about thirty minutes until all the soapsuds had disappeared. Any spots he could not reach with his hand he worked on with a cotton swab. It was very important to remove all the oil from both birds and otters. An oily spot smaller than a quarter would expose the animals to the freezing waters of the sound and rapidly lead to hypothermia and death. Adkins also removed ticks from the bird's head with a tweezers.

When the animals were clean, they were held in pens and cages to fully recuperate. Otters groomed their fur to stimulate the production of sebum. Fresh lobster and shellfish were flown in daily, compliments of Exxon, for the otters to eat. Similar processes, with teams of up to four people working on one animal, took place all around Prince William Sound.

For some people, the animal rescue experience was difficult to bear. Georgiana Ruff, a travel agent who volunteered at one of the animal rehabilitation clinics, learned to care for the animals. But most of them were too ill for treatment and subsequently died. Frustrated by her inability to help the animals, she quit the clinic. She explained her reasons: "To hear those animals screaming in pain—it's just awful. I would dream about that sound. I would have had a nervous breakdown if I'd kept on with it."

Many Did Not Survive

While many animals were saved, many did not survive. One third of the birds—approximately 1,900— and half the otters—around 200— died. This was usually due to irreversible damage to livers, lungs, and kidneys. In the end, 627 birds and about 200 otters were saved. The process was expensive. Considering

Volunteers painstakingly wash the oil from a puffin. Many volunteers took time off from their jobs to help rehabilitate wildlife victims of the oil spill.

the cost of staff, ships, facilities, supplies, and food, each otter that survived cost Exxon about $40,000. The small number of birds and otters saved seems especially insignificant when compared to the numbers that died: 7,000 otters and at least 100,000 birds.

After four months, most of the rehabilitated animals were ready to be returned to their homes. But their homes were still covered with oil, and animal experts did not want to risk having the cleaned animals covered with oil again. Migratory birds, which would fly away, were released. Territorial birds and otters were held in their cages for the winter, to wait for the storms of the season to clean their beaches in a way that human beings could not.

Whether the animal rescue efforts were a success is debatable. Peter Fitzmaurice, chief ranger at Kenai Fjords National Park, believes that cleaning the animals helped people feel better after the trauma of watching so much pristine natural beauty soiled. He said,

> The oil spill is a really emotional thing up here, and a lot of people wanted to do something to feel like they're making it better. For purely emotional reasons it's really uplifting to watch birds and otters come in dirty on one end and watch them come out clean on the other end. It's been uplifting for me.

However, Fitzmaurice continued:

> From the cold, hard, biological viewpoint, the rescue can't be seen as of much value [to the animal population] at all.

Fishers Hard-Hit by Oil Slick

The fishing industry was also deeply affected by the spill. For fishers, fishing is not only a source of income, it also repays debts from buying expensive ships and supplies. Max McCarty is a fisher from Cordova, a community hit hard by the oil slick. He described himself as an "average little guy" and explained why he loves the life of a fisher and why the oil spill was hard on him. From his boat, the *Christina*

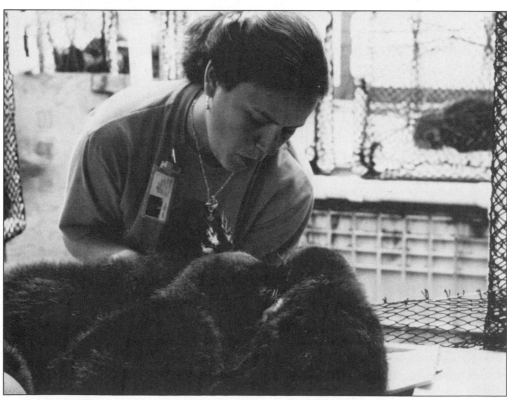

An animal rehabilitation worker feeds three young, freshly scrubbed sea otters that were fortunate enough to have been rescued from an oily fate.

Fishing trawlers set their nets off the coast of Alaska. Vital to Alaska's economy, the fishing industry suffered heavy losses from the Exxon oil spill.

Sue, he looked at the snow-capped mountains around him:

> Look where I work. I have the finest scenery in the world. I don't care who you are, you gotta appreciate this. We were expecting forty million salmon in Prince William Sound this year. This was going to be a good year. Vacation. Fix up the house. All winter long you think about this good year coming, and now you wonder what's going to happen.

McCarty blamed Exxon for spilling the oil and for not cleaning it up quickly enough. "The bottom line is, we're screwed," said McCarty. "There's no way you can win, dealing with Exxon."

Most other fishers shared Mc-Carty's feelings that Exxon was to blame for their misfortune. In Cordova, angry fishers confronted an Exxon representative at a press conference. Fishers carried signs that read "Exxon Double Cross" and "Don't Believe What You Hear." One by one, they marched up to the microphone or simply stood up where they were to shout what was on their minds.

Bribe or Opportunity?

Fishers disagreed over how to act in the face of the spill. Some believed that taking money from Exxon, which they thought was trying to cover its mistake by spending a lot on the fishers and other

Three young native Alaskans wait atop the family fishing boat to see whether they will be able to go out to fish. The oil spill deprived many native people of their traditional livelihood.

Alaskans, was wrong. They thought Exxon was trying to bribe them, and believed that people should voluntarily help clean up.

Others saw it as an opportunity to make the money they could not make fishing. They charged Exxon as much as $8,000 per day to use their boats for cleanup and animal rescue crews. These people were disparagingly labeled "spillionaires" by fishers who thought the behavior was unethical.

The Spill's Effect on Natives

Commercial fishers were not the only ones whose livelihood was impaired by the damage to the fish. The Chugach-Aleut natives also collect most of their food from the wa-ters of the sound. When the spill occurred, a thousand or so natives had their hunting grounds oiled.

It's Scary

In one village, Tatitlek, near Bligh Reef, a village elder named Ed Gregorieff expressed concern. "Right now, herring are spawning. The salmon and ducks are coming in. It's scary because we don't know what's happening."

Exxon's and the state's immediate response was to send groceries to the natives. But the native Alaskans preferred their traditional food of fish, clams, and mussels. Exxon began to ship in fresh salmon from other areas of Alaska. Other native communities, hearing of the misfortune of places like Tatitlek, sent shellfish and other traditional food.

One native man was distressed because the oily water prevented his people from gathering their own food as they had done for centuries. He feared that his people would stop gathering the fish and clams and rely on food shipped into the community. "How can the young learn our ways," he asked, "when the water is dead?"

Natives, environmentalists, animal lovers, fishers, and average people looked for someone to blame for the spill, and Exxon was usually identified as being the most

A native Alaskan man prepares to smoke salmon. Native people who live along the coast of Alaska depend on salmon for food. They worried about the impact the oil spill would have on the fishing season.

responsible party. However, in the days immediately after his ship ran aground, Captain Joseph Hazelwood was the one person many saw as the perpetrator of the largest oil spill in Alaskan history.

From the morning his ship collided with Bligh Reef, Joseph Hazelwood was at the center of public attention. For many people, Hazelwood was the single person most responsible for the spill. There was some evidence that Hazelwood had been drinking before boarding the ship, and some speculation that he was drunk when it ran aground. In fact, the day after the spill, the *New York Post*'s headlines screamed,

"Skipper Was Drunk."

In late March, Hazelwood returned to his Huntington Bay, New York, home. Because his photograph was widely published in American newspapers, he had recently shaved his beard when he was arrested and charged with four crimes: criminal mischief, operating a vessel while intoxicated, reckless endangerment, and negligent discharge of oil. Hazelwood faced a possible seven years in prison and $61,000 in fines if found guilty of all four. He was set free on bail, and returned to his home until the trial.

The trial was held at the Superior Court Building in Anchorage. It be-

Exxon Valdez skipper Joseph Hazelwood (right) sits quietly by his attorney during his trial in February 1990. A jury found Hazelwood guilty of negligent discharge of oil but innocent of operating his ship while drunk.

gan in early February 1990. During the two months it lasted, the prosecution sought to prove that Hazelwood had been drinking at the Pipeline Club in Valdez and on the ship, and that his drunkenness caused the wreck of the *Exxon Valdez*. Hazelwood's lawyers, one of them a college friend, brought witnesses to testify that Hazelwood did not appear to be impaired when he left the Pipeline Club or while on board ship. Even witnesses for the prosecution testified that Hazelwood did not act like he was drunk or under the influence of alcohol. Hazelwood did not testify. Throughout the trial, he showed little emotion.

Never Testified at Trial

Because the harbor pilot thought he had smelled alcohol on Hazelwood's breath the night of the last voyage of the *Exxon Valdez*, Hazelwood was tested when he left the ship nine hours after it ran aground. The test showed that his blood alcohol level was 0.06 of 1 percent, or that six hundredths of one percent of his blood was alcohol. This level exceeded the Coast Guard's limit of 0.04 of 1 percent, but fell short of the state's limit of 0.10 of 1 percent. It is not known what Hazelwood's blood alcohol level was at the time his ship ran aground. Because Hazelwood never testified at the trial, it is not known whether he was drunk or not when the *Exxon Valdez* left the port that night, or if he drank during the nine hours after the ship ran aground and before he was

tested.

Hazelwood had twice lost his driver's license in his home state of New York for driving under the influence of alcohol. Exxon had been aware that Hazelwood had had drinking problems in the past, and fired him as soon as they received the test results after the spill.

Another piece of information disclosed at the trial was that both Second Mate Cousins and Helmsman Robert Kagan were very inexperienced. Kagan had been promoted from his position as food server and room steward to the crucial position of helmsman only one year before the accident. A deck officer from the *Exxon Valdez* testified that Kagan "does the best he can, but you have to watch him."

Cousins testified that because of his own inexperience, Second Mate Lloyd LeCain was supposed to relieve him on the bridge shortly after Hazelwood handed those duties over to him. However, since LeCain had recently finished a long shift and was asleep, Cousins did not wish to wake him. LeCain said that if he had gone on duty when he was scheduled to, he would have replaced Kagan with a more experienced helmsman because of Kagan's unfamiliarity with the sometimes difficult maneuvers required in the sea lanes leading to and from the port of Valdez.

Not Guilty

On March 22, 1990, a jury of six women and six men found Hazelwood not guilty on all but the least

THE WEATHERING PROCESS OF OIL

The crude oil that leaked out of the *Exxon Valdez* began to change almost immediately, as it reacted with the air and water.

Some of the oil formed microscopic droplets and sank through the water to the seafloor. This natural process is the same one that chemical dispersants try to imitate.

As much as 25 percent of the oil evaporated naturally into the air. A few of the lighter components in the oil dissolved in the waters of the sound. This process occurred during the first two weeks of the spill.

When the lighter elements disap-peared, the remaining oil became thick and sticky. Waves stirred the heavier elements into a mousse, a combination of oil and water virtually impossible for cleanup crews to pump.

Microorganisms further degraded the oil until it became tar balls, which washed ashore between one and three months after the spill. In some areas tar balls that had washed ashore would melt during warm days and then reharden into rigid tar during the night. Some of this oil was cleaned up by Exxon-funded cleanup crews. Most of it was removed by natural processes.

Ugly black tar balls and barnacles cling to the rocky shore. Tar balls are left after oil from a spill degrades from the action of wind, water, and bacteria.

serious charge: negligent discharge of oil. Most significantly, they found no evidence that Hazelwood was drunk or that his judgment was impaired by alcohol.

Bursts of applause erupted in the courthouse when the verdict was read. Many people felt that Hazelwood had been made a scapegoat for the spill. Juror Jeffrey Sage, a convenience store manager, said, "No law states Hazelwood had to be on the bridge [when in Prince William Sound]. Hazelwood made no mistakes. His only bad judgment was leaving the bridge."

Alaskan superior court Judge Karl Johnstone, who seemed irritated that Hazelwood had not shown more remorse for the tragedy, imposed the maximum sentence of one thousand hours of community service cleaning the rocky beaches of Prince William Sound, and ordered him to pay $58,500 restitution to the state for court and legal costs.

Exxon quit its multi-million dollar cleanup effort in September 1989, without succeeding in "picking up, one way or another, all the oil that was out there." Some of the shorelines were completely cleaned, but most had a layer of tar an inch thick or more just below the surface. This tar, and all the other remnants of the oil spill that Exxon left behind, continue to be cleaned by the action of the winter wind and waves.

During the winter, attention shifted away from the spill. Instead, environmentalists and Alaskans turned their energies toward preventing and preparing for future oil spills.

Five

Could It Happen Again?

Oil continues to be pumped from the Valdez area. And, since it is unlikely that the energy needs of the United States will decrease, oil will continue to be pumped from the area. The question remains, however, as to whether another oil spill as large as the one from the *Exxon Valdez* could ever happen again.

In an effort to prevent such a recurrence, Alaska's governor Steve Cowper formed the Alaska Oil Spill Commission (AOSC) shortly after the spill. The AOSC's purpose was to investigate the causes of the accident and to make recommendations to prevent another such accident from happening. The commission's report, issued in January 1990, recommended several significant changes in the way the oil industry operates in Valdez.

Noting that safety standards had deteriorated before the spill, the AOSC recommended appointing an independent group of volunteer citizens and environmentalists to oversee safety standards set by the Alaskan government. The commission felt that civilians would be more objective at evaluating oil operations than the oil companies themselves. In addition, civilians would not hesitate to institute improvements, whereas oil companies might decide such improvements were too expensive.

In support of this recommendation, Alyeska donated two million dollars a year to its operation. The volunteer group will use part of this money to further study the effects of oil on the sound and to research new cleanup methods.

The AOSC also recommended new standards for cleanup operations. Because of the slow and confused response to the *Exxon Valdez* spill, the AOSC recommended the creation of spill-fighting teams called regional spill-response units. The AOSC stated that these units should be set up like fire departments to be able to respond quickly to oil spills.

Quick Response to Oil Spills

In June 1989, the oil industry created the Petroleum Industry Response Organization (PIRO) to form the cleanup teams the AOSC envisioned. PIRO established five regional centers for fighting oil spills. Located at various places along the U.S. coastline, the centers

The *Exxon Baton Rouge* pumps oil from the damaged *Exxon Valdez* in an attempt to stop it from leaking into Prince William Sound. Alaskans now wonder what they can do to prevent or minimize the damage from possible future accidents.

Exxon Shipping Company president Frank Iarossi talks to reporters about the condition of the *Exxon Valdez* and how best to deal with future oil spills.

provide a quick response to oil spills across the entire United States. The petroleum industry contributed over seven million dollars to create these centers. Although they cannot always respond as quickly as a fire department, they are staffed twenty-four hours a day and are equipped to handle spills of up to two hundred thousand barrels. In Alaska, Alyeska's spill-response team has also been improved to allow it to respond speedily to a large spill. It received new equipment, and its round-the-clock status has been resumed.

The AOSC also recommended changes in the responsibility for oil spill cleanup. It concluded that the federal government, and not the company that spilled the oil, should be in charge of the cleanup. The AOSC believed that a centralized authority such as a government agency could have moved cleanup crews onto the water faster and prevented some of the oil from reaching the shore.

Exxon Shipping Company president Frank Iarossi agrees that authority should be centralized. In the event of an oil spill, he recommends that a "dictator" with unquestioned authority be appointed. "You need somebody on the scene with authority to act," says Iarossi. But many in the oil industry feel that the government is not the right choice for this "dictator." They argue that the government is incapable of mustering resources or spending enough money to fight a large spill. These critics argue that an oil company like Exxon has yearly profits totalling in the billions. A government agency, at the most, could be funded with a few million dollars. In addition, government agencies are constantly subjected to cutbacks, whereas private cleanup operations could be funded consistently. To date, this issue remains undecided.

Double Hulls

In further recommendations, the AOSC stated emphatically that "double hulls . . . should be required." Many people agree with this sentiment, including former Exxon tanker crew member Arthur McKenzie. McKenzie, now director of the Tanker Advisory Center in New York, an organization that monitors the world's tankers, states that of thirty-two hundred tankers in the world, only five have double hulls.

McKenzie cites two examples of these hulls' effectiveness. In one, a double-hulled ship carrying liquefied natural gas ran aground off the coast of Japan, where 40 percent of its hull was damaged. Another double-hulled ship with the same cargo hit some rocks on the bottom of the Straits of Gibraltar and was so badly damaged that repairs took fifteen months. But "neither one spilled a drop of cargo," said McKenzie.

Too Expensive

Most oil companies say that double-hulled tankers are too expensive to build. A Coast Guard report, however, found that the cost of a double-hulled tanker, spread out over an estimated life of twenty years, would probably be as low as three cents per barrel of oil. Another study showed that a double hull on the *Exxon Valdez* could have cut the oil loss by 60 percent, or 150,000 gallons.

At least one oil company, Conoco, believes in the AOSC's recommendations. In 1990, Conoco announced its intention to begin building its new tankers with double hulls. The president of Conoco, Constantine S. Nicandros, believes that petroleum transport is becoming more hazardous, and therefore that safer tankers are more important than ever. "It is certain," he said, "that our nation faces increased tanker traffic due to the growing dependency on foreign oil,

and more traffic demands better ships to reduce risks from transportation of crude oil." However, Congress passed no laws requiring double-hulled tankers.

New Laws

In addition to the recommendations of the AOSC, Alaska state legislators passed laws to avoid a future spill. Most of these laws concern how the tankers are operated, particularly in Prince William Sound. For example, the state strengthened standards for tanker personnel. As a result of the controversy surrounding Joseph Hazelwood, all tanker captains leaving port are now required to take a breath alcohol test within one hour before boarding their ships. If a captain fails the test, or refuses to take it, he or she is not allowed to board.

Tankers must also keep two pilots on the bridge until a point past Bligh Reef. They must also be accompanied by two tugboats while they are in the sound. This policy paid off within six months of the grounding of the *Exxon Valdez*. On September 20, 1989, a ship called the *Antigun Pass*, carrying forty million gallons of crude oil, was sailing through the sound toward the treacherous Bligh Reef when its engines failed. One of the escort tugboats hooked up a towline and pulled the ship off its collision course with the reef until it regained power. Thus the new guidelines averted a second collision and oil spill.

Also, tanker pilots are no longer

ALTERNATIVE FORMS OF ENERGY

The *Exxon Valdez* oil spill renewed cries by environmentalists and others for a search for alternative forms of energy. Oil and coal, both fossil fuels, are the two most common forms of energy in the United States. But drilling oil and mining coal damage the surface of the land, and burning them pollutes the air.

Some means of generating energy have existed for centuries. For instance, the windmills of Holland have used the wind's power to mill grain and perform other tasks for hundreds of years. Modern wind generators provide small amounts of energy, but can only be used in limited areas.

Water is another traditional source for generating power. In ancient times, the current in streams and rivers was used to turn waterwheels that milled grain or sawed wood. Today, huge dams use a similar technique to generate electricity. Some countries such as Norway and Zaire produce over 95 percent of their energy by using water power. Dams generate only 14 percent of the electricity in the United States. Experts generally agree that the United States is using as much of its water power as is available.

The sun is another possible energy source. Unfortunately, the technology to harness this energy has not yet been developed. On a small scale, solar collectors can harness enough energy for heating and cooling a house or a small building. However, solar collectors cannot presently be used to generate energy on a large scale.

Nuclear power was developed in the 1940s, and provides 20 percent of the electricity generated in the United States. In the northeast United States, nuclear reactors provide 50 percent of the electricity. Stephen Binney of Oregon State University is an expert on nuclear power. He has demonstrated that nuclear reactors could supply all of the United States' energy needs well into the twenty-first century. The disadvantage of nuclear power is the possibility of a nuclear accident. Even a small accident could release deadly radioactive steam into the atmosphere. And a large accident, called a meltdown, would release even more deadly radioactive particles into the air. Such an accident could kill thousands. Though a total meltdown is highly unlikely, many people feel that nuclear power is not worth the risk. So it has not been developed to its full potential in the United States.

Concrete domes house the nuclear reactors of a power plant.

Crew members assemble solar panels.

A cleanup worker monitors a skimmer that removes spilled oil from the surface of the sea. The conveyor moves the oil onto a barge for storage.

allowed to change lanes and must never exceed a maximum speed of ten knots (slightly more than eleven and a half miles per hour). The *Exxon Valdez* routinely traveled at a speed of twelve knots (almost fourteen miles per hour).

Although these changes have improved chances that another accident can be averted in Prince William Sound, standards for tankers transporting oil and other liquid fuels around other parts of the United States have changed little.

And even in Prince William Sound, an accident is still possible. A Coast Guard study has shown that 85 percent of all tanker accidents are the result of human error. Even with improved safety standards, tanker captains could still make mistakes that lead to accidents.

And when humans fail, methods for removing spilled oil from the water have improved little since the 1950s. Though the five regional response centers somewhat increase the availability of equipment for cleaning up and removing oil spills, the oil from a large spill, like that from the *Exxon Valdez*, can quickly overwhelm the limited amount of equipment each regional spill center has. Days would pass before additional equipment from another center could arrive. For example, the center closest to the one in Alaska is on the coast of Washington state. Oil would spread to shorelines before enough equipment was

THE ARCTIC NATIONAL WILDLIFE REFUGE

The Arctic National Wildlife Refuge, or ANWR, lies sixty miles east of the Prudhoe Bay oil fields. Because it is home for a large herd of caribou, it is protected from development by the federal government. Under the ground, however, the U.S. Department of the Interior estimates that there is as much as nine billion barrels of crude oil. That is almost as much oil as was discovered at Prudhoe Bay, where half the reserves have been pumped. Oil from ANWR could also be pumped down the Trans-Alaska Pipeline to Valdez.

In the search for domestic oil, a U.S. Senate committee approved a bill allowing oil and gas drilling in ANWR shortly before the *Exxon Valdez* ran aground. After the accident, public opinion was so strong against the oil industry that the bill was not even introduced to the Senate. Foster Mellen, an analyst with a Washington, D.C. petroleum consulting firm, said that the spill "means that development of the refuge reserves will be pushed further down the road—if [it is done] at all."

However, in view of the nation's huge need for domestic oil, many people feel that development of ANWR is inevitable. Charles DiBona, president of the American Petroleum Institute, believes that Americans would much rather drill for oil in the ANWR than import it from Saudi Arabia. With huge reserves of untapped oil in ANWR, it is probable that oil will continue to flow through the pipeline for years to come. It is certain that the debate weighing the benefits of domestic oil against the risk to the environment will continue just as long.

A herd of caribou grazes peacefully in the Arctic National Wildlife Refuge in northern Alaska. The refuge's legal immunity to development may be lifted to allow oil companies to tap the refuge's huge underground oil reserves.

present to remove it. If another spill as big as the one from the *Exxon Valdez* occurs, beaches will still be oiled and wildlife will still suffer and die.

Because of the great danger of another oil spill, and the inadequacies of even the best cleanup and oil-removal technology, some experts believe there must be more restrictions on oil transport. For example, the commissioner of the Alaska Department of Environmental Conservation, Dennis Kelso, believes that tanker travel should be suspended when weather conditions would not permit oil spill cleanup.

Even with improved safeguards, human beings in control of the ships can, and will, make mistakes. Considering the hundreds of ships in use every day, another major oil spill may be inevitable.

Suggestions for Further Reading

Jerry Adler, "The Cleanup Is Ending and the Beaches Are Still Fouled." *Newsweek*, September 18, 1989.

Marcia Barinaga, "Alaskan Oil Spill: Health Risks Uncovered." *Science*, August 4, 1989.

Richard Behar, "Joe's Bad Trip." *Time*, July 24, 1989.

Mary Clay Berry, *The Alaska Pipeline*. Bloomington, Indiana, and London: Indiana University Press, 1975.

Kaj Birket-Smith, *The Chugach Eskimo*. Copenhagen, Denmark: Nationalmuseets Publikationsfond, 1953.

Barry Came, "Tragedy on a Reef." *Maclean's*, April 3, 1989.

George J. Church, "The Big Spill." *Time*, April 10, 1989.

Bryan Cooper, *Alaska: The Last Frontier*. New York: William Morrow and Company, Inc., 1973.

Lisa Drew, "Truth or Consequences Along Oiled Shores." *National Wildlife*, June/July 1990.

Jennifer Reed Gilliland, "Moving Alaskan Crude: Who's in Charge?" *Audubon*, September 1989.

Willian Glasgall and Vicky Cahan, "Questions That Keep Surfacing after the Spill." *Business Week*, April 17, 1989.

Frank Graham, Jr., "Oilspeak, Common Sense, and Soft Science." *Audobon*, September 1989.

Linden Gross, "Valdez: One Family's Story." *Ladies' Home Journal*, April 1990.

Bryan Hodgson, "Alaska's Big Spill: Can the Wilderness Heal?" *National Geographic*, January 1990.

"Hydroelectric Power." *Academic American Encyclopedia*, New York: Grolier, 1990.

"In Ten Years You'll See 'Nothing'." *Fortune*, May 8, 1989.

Dorothy M. Jones, *Aleuts in Transition*. Seattle and London: University of Washington Press, 1976.

George Laycock, "The Baptism of Prince William Sound." *Audubon*, September 1989.

George Laycock, "The Disaster That Won't Go Away." *Audubon*, September 1990.

Jon R. Luoma, "Terror and Triage at the Laundry." *Audubon*, September 1989.

Peter Nulty, "Is Exxon's Muck-Up at Valdez a Reason to Ban Drilling in One of the Industry's Hottest Prospects? *Fortune*, May 8, 1989.

Leslie Roberts, "Long, Slow Recovery Predicted for Alaska." *Science*, April 7, 1989.

George W. Rogers, *Alaska in Transition: The Southeast Region*. Baltimore: The Johns Hopkins Press, 1960.

Andrea Rothman, David Castellon, and Sandra D. Atchinson, "Who's That Screaming at Exxon? Not the Environmentalists." *Business Week*, May 1, 1989.

Benjamin Shwadran, *Middle East Oil Crises Since 1973*. Boulder, Colorado: Westview Press, 1986.

Nora Underwood, "A Captain's Guilt." *Maclean's*, April 2, 1990.

Paul A. Witteman, "Fall Guy or Villain?" *Time*, February 26, 1990.

Paul A. Witteman, "First Mess Up, Then Mop Up," *Time*, April 2, 1990.

Index

Picture Credits

Cover: Brian McGovern, McGovern Graphics

AP/Wide World Photos, 11, 21, 25, 28 (bottom), 29, 46, 52, 55
© Alissa Crandall, 9, 23
Division of Tourism, Alaska, 13, 32
International Bird Rescue Research Center, 38, 41
Library of Congress, 10, 14 (bottom)
© Richard Newman, 33, 48
© Joseph L. Paris, 54 (left)
Sperry Marine, Inc., 19
UPI/Bettmann, 51
U.S. Coast Guard, 43, 54
U.S. Department of Interior, 56
U.S. Fish and Wildlife Service, 30, 31 (bottom), 37, 39
© 1989 Vanessa Vick, 28 (top), 31 (top), 35, 42, 44, 45

About the Author

The author, Tom Schouweiler, is a free-lance writer who was raised in Marine on St. Croix, Minnesota. He currently lives in St. Paul, Minnesota. This is his third book.